LIVING WITH ALBINISM

LIVING WITH ALBINISM

By Elaine Landau

A FIRST BOOK

FRANKLIN WATTS   A Division of Grolier Publishing
New York / London / Hong Kong / Sydney / Danbury, Connecticut

LIVING
WITH
ALBINISM

FOR MICHAEL

Interior and cover design: Michelle Regan
Cover illustration ©: Victoria Vebell

Photographs ©: Ben Klaffke: 10, 14 bottom left, 18, 19, 22, 24, 44, 47, 51; Custom Medical Stock Photo: 25 top, 29, 31; Eschenbach: 26, 27; Photo Researchers: 21, 36, 38, 43, 11 top (Tim Davis), 14 center right (Tom & Pat Leeson), 11 bottom (Jeff Lepore), 14 top left (Tom McHugh); The Field Museum, Chicago, IL: 15; Visuals Unlimited: 14 bottom right (Ken Lucas), 14 top right (Karl Maslowski), 12, 23 (Joe McDonald), 25 bottom (Kjell B. Sandved), 13 (Ken Wagner).

Library of Congress Cataloging-in-Publication Data

Landau, Elaine.
Living with albinism / by Elaine Landau.
p.   cm. — (A First book)
Includes bibliographical references and index.
Summary: Describes albinism, the inherited condition in which the individual lacks or has a shortage of melanin, the substance responsible for the body's coloring.
ISBN 0-531-20296-8
1. Albinos and albinism—Juvenile literature.   [1. Albinos and albinism.]
I. Title. II. Series.
RL790.L36 1997
616.5'5—DC21   97-1771
                                                                 CIP
                                                                 AC

Visit Franklin Watts on the Internet at:
http://publishing.grolier.com

CONTENTS

CHAPTER 1

WHAT IS ALBINISM?

In many ways, Ariel, an eleven-year-old girl from Massachusetts, is very much like her two closest friends. All three girls like going to the mall, buying new clothes, and talking on the phone for hours. But while the members of this tireless trio are all about the same height and weight, Ariel looks different from her friends in some ways. She doesn't have her mother's flaming red hair or her father's dark brown eyes, either.

A twelve-year-old girl with albinism

Ariel's coloring differs sharply from that of her family members and friends. She has extremely pale skin, light-blue eyes, and white hair. At times, Ariel has been told that she looks like a heavenly angel—but she also has been called a "ghost." In reality, Ariel is neither. She is simply a young girl with **albinism**.

A Lack of Pigment

Albinism is the term used to describe a number of inherited conditions in which an individual either lacks or has a shortage of **melanin**, a **pigment**. A variety of pigments cause the broad range of colors in animals and nature. Pigments are responsible for the red feathers of a robin's breast, for example. Melanin is a brown pigment responsible for skin, hair, and eye color in humans. Different people have varying amounts of melanin. Those with fair complexions have less melanin than African Americans and other people of color.

Pigments are responsible for the various colors we see in different animals.

A man with albinism from Bangalore, India, is shown here with his wife.

People with albinism usually have little or no coloring in their skin, eyes, and hair. They generally have some problems with their eyesight as well. There are different forms of albinism, and the condition affects about 1 person out of every 17,000. Most children with albinism have parents with average coloring.

Albinism occurs not only in humans, but also in animals and plants. Many albino animals, such as white horses or white ducks, are really partial albinos, as they have some pigment or color in their eyes, beaks, or legs. In partial-albino plants, the blossoms or flowers are white, while the stems and leaves are green. On a full albino plant, however, even the stems and leaves are white. Such plants usually do not live very long, since they lack **chlorophyll**—the green substance necessary for plants to manufacture food.

Notice how both the stem and the leaves are white in this full albino plant.

Albinism affects animals as well as humans throughout the world.

A young Hopi Indian child with albinism stands against a building with two other Hopi girls. Children with albinism were once cherished by the Hopi people.

Old Attitudes

Albinism is not new. It has appeared throughout history in cultures around the world. It affects people of all races and ethnic groups. Some think that albinism may be the oldest-recorded **inherited** condition. Nevertheless, albinism has often been extremely misunderstood. Depending on the time, place, and circumstances, people with albinism have sometimes been either worshipped or scorned.

For example, studies conducted by Charles Woolf and Frank Dukepoo of Arizona State University revealed that before the early 1900s, people with albinism were held in high esteem by the Hopi Indians of Arizona. These researchers found that people with albinism were considered "smart, clean, and pretty" and often became chiefs and priests within the tribe. The birth of a child with albinism was joyously welcomed. According to the study,

15

having a large number of people with albinism in the village was highly desirable as their coloring "was seen as a sign of . . . purity." [1]

This book is about what it's like to be a young person with albinism today. It reveals the facts about what has sometimes been considered a mysterious condition.

CHAPTER 2

ALBINISM AND ITS EFFECTS

*T*here is nothing mysterious or supernatural about albinism. It is neither a blessing nor a curse sent by God, but rather a group of inherited conditions that occur under specific circumstances. Children inherit albinism from their parents. It is passed on to them through defective *genes* that do not make the usual amounts of the pigment melanin.

While this young Latino boy has albinism, his parents have average coloring.

How Albinism Occurs

In most forms of albinism, both parents have to carry the gene for the child to be born with the condition. In many such families, the gene has been passed from generation to generation with no one showing any sign of albinism or even realizing that he or she is a **carrier**. But if such a person has a child with someone who also has the gene, there is a 25 percent chance that their baby will have albinism. In cases in which both parents—along with everyone else in their families—have average coloring, the birth of a baby with albinism can come as a shock.

The odds change when a person with albinism has a child with someone who does not have the condition. If the spouse of the person with albinism is not carrying the gene for albinism, the child will be a carrier, but will not have albinism. If, however, the spouse has the gene for albinism, there is a 50 percent chance that the child will have albinism.

These rules of heredity do not apply to a particular form of albinism known as X-linked ocular albinism. This form of albinism

In this family from India, the mother has albinism, while her son and husband have average coloring.

is passed from mothers to sons. Although females carry the gene, it is males who most often exhibit the condition. Nevertheless, the mothers of these children often show some pigmentary (color) differences in their eyes. Their **retinas** have a mixture of pigmented and uncolored areas.

Until recently, there was no way of knowing for certain whether someone was a carrier for albinism. But now there is a blood test that identifies carriers for some types of albinism. Still another test can tell if a fetus (unborn child) will have albinism.

Types of Albinism

The different types of albinism vary in severity and in how they affect the body. As medical research continues, scientists are identifying additional forms of albinism and their effects as well. So far, researchers have isolated numerous kinds of **oculocutaneous** albinism, which affect a person's eyes, skin, and hair. In one severe type, affected individuals have no melanin whatsoever. Many of these people have serious vision problems. In another, milder form, individuals have some pigment and so generally have less difficulty with their sight.

Scientists have pinpointed at least five different types of a second kind of albinism known as **ocular** albinism. Ocular albinism affects mainly the person's eyes, but sometimes the individual's hair and skin may be lighter as well.

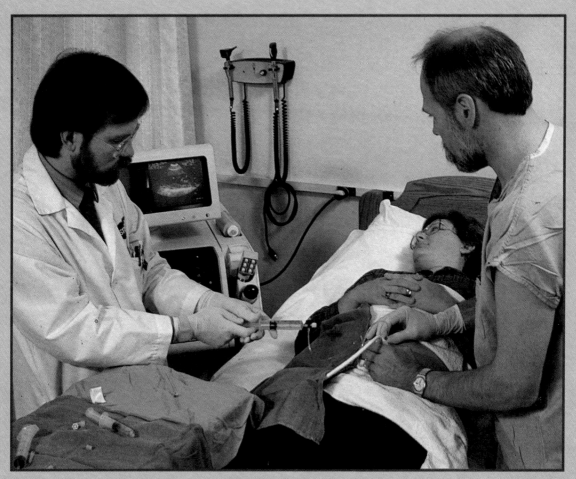

Today, a test can determine if an unborn child will have albinism.

Eye Problems

The eye problems resulting from albinism occur because the eye doesn't develop normally due to the lack of pigment. The most common vision difficulties are nearsightedness, farsightedness, strabismus (one or both eyes turning inward or outward), and nystagmus (involuntary rapid jerky movements of the eyeballs).

Albinism can result in a number of different vision problems.

People with albinism also find that their eyes are extremely sensitive to bright light and glare. As one woman described how she and others with albinism react to various forms of light:

> As for bright light, we have to keep a balance. Light too bright (bright sunlight or new snow) will blind us—not permanently of course. Indoor light can be disturbing to a very small child [with albinism]. [A] child may squint, close his eyes, look down, any number of things to let you know he is uncomfortable. But we need light in order to see. Contrary to popular thought, we do not function well in dimly lit or dark rooms. We cannot see in the dark. Each of us learns to adjust to whatever suits us best. Some of us wear tinted glasses, hats or visors. Some of us squint or blink a lot without realizing it. [A] child will find his own comfort level and will learn to make friends with the light.[1]

This man's eyes are extremely sensitive to light. Notice how he squints in the sun's bright glare.

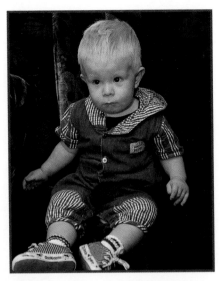

Many people with albinism have light-blue or blue-grey eyes.

Some people mistakenly think that everyone with albinism has red or pink eyes. But people with albinism are actually more likely to have light-blue or blue-grey eyes. In some types of albinism, the individual's eyes may seem to have a violet or reddish tint. However, according to eye specialist Dr. James Haefemeyer, "The reddish color comes from the retina in the back of the eye. In people with lighter complexions, the retina has less pigment. Most of the arteries and veins behind the retina show through. . . . Therefore the reddish eyes of a person with albinism are actually just reflecting the red blood vessels from the back of the eye through the iris [the part of the eye that is usually colored]." Dr. Haefemeyer further notes, "In rabbits the iris is very thin and the retina very red, so the eyes look red. In humans the iris is usually thick enough that this happens only a little." [2]

Optical Aids

People with albinism often rely on various **optical aids** to improve their sight. Depending on their needs, they may use eyeglasses, contact lenses, a magnifying glass, or

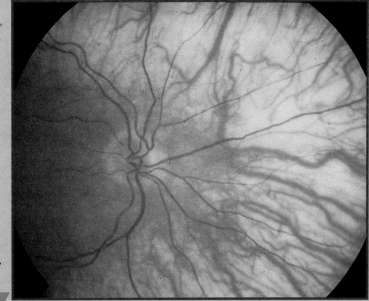

An internal view of the eye of a person with albinism

The eyes of this ferret look red because they have thin irises and very red retinas.

This hand-held telescope makes reading charts and graphs easier.

Here a miniature telescope placed directly in the lower portion of an eyeglass lens enhances the wearer's vision.

a small, specially designed hand-held telescope, as well as other devices. The type of optical aid needed by someone with albinism varies from person to person. As there are significant differences in vision and the kinds of work done by people with albinism, it is crucial that any optical aid be precisely tailored to the individual's needs. Miniature telescopes provide a clearer view of a distant object. Hand-held telescopes come in a variety of shapes and sizes, while very tiny telescopes can be clipped onto a pair of glasses. There's also a "behind-the-lens" telescope that can placed on either the right or left of the lower portion of an eyeglass lens.

Among the most beneficial optical aids for someone with albinism is a closed-circuit television (CCTV). Such a device, which may be used for either work or school, magnifies written materials and can be adjusted to the viewer's needs. CCTV can be especially helpful to students for reading charts and graphs, as well as text. However, it is less portable than glasses or small magnifiers, and it is considerably more costly.

The optical needs of someone with albinism may change with the passage of time. New designs and various technological advances are always on the horizon as well. At times an individual may own several optical aids, each one geared specifically for a special task.

Sun-Sensitive Skin

People with albinism have a normal life span and usually experience the same illnesses and other medical conditions as the general population. However, their fair, sensitive skin must be protected from the sun to avoid sunburn and various types of skin cancer. When in the sun, it is important for people with albinism to use a sun screen with a **sun protection factor** (SPF) of at least 20 or 30. A product's SPF indicates how long a person can remain in the sun without burning.

Overexposure to the sun can be a problem for those with albinism.

Yet many people who use sunscreens may not really be getting as much protection as they think. Most individuals use only a small amount of lotion on themselves, thinking that's enough. But they are actually using only a fraction of what is used in laboratory tests to determine sunscreen protection.

Proper Use of Sunscreen

The National Organization for Albinism and Hypopigmentation (NOAH) notes that an adult should use about 1 ounce (30 ml) of sunscreen with each application. Since sunscreen is often purchased in 4-ounce (120-ml) bottles, everyone—whether or not they have albinism—should use about a quarter of the bottle each time the sunscreen is applied. Unfortunately, many people who expose themselves to strong sun rays every day use only one bottle of sunscreen during an entire summer.

It is equally important that sunscreen be applied to all parts of the body exposed to the sun. Spots commonly missed include the tops of ears and the backs of arms and legs. The National Organization for Albinism and Hypopigmentation further stresses that bikers should apply sunscreen to their lower backs, since their shirts often ride up while biking.

In recent years, there has been some debate about how high a sunscreen's SPF must be to provide adequate pro-

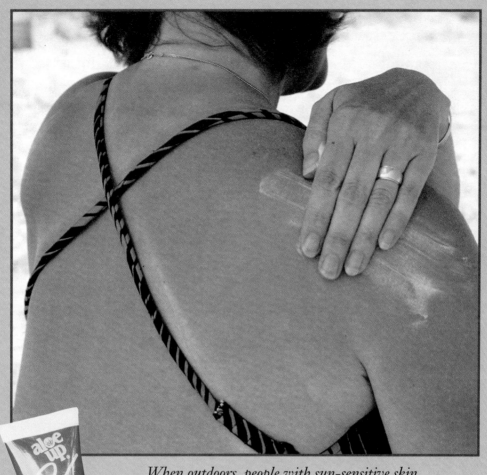

When outdoors, people with sun-sensitive skin should use sunscreen with a high SPF.

tection. Some magazine advertisements for sunscreens with an SPF of 15 state that anything higher is unnecessary and that in using those products "you only put more chemicals on your skin." The National Organization for Albinism and Hypopigmentation asserts, however, that this isn't necessarily so for those with albinism or others with sun-sensitive skin.

The group points to the work of Dr. Madhu A. Pathak, a leading university authority on the subject. According to Dr. Pathak, "Sun-sensitive people . . . may derive additional benefits of assured protection by using such products with high SPF values of 20 and 30, but these sun-sensitive individuals are vulnerable and should not indulge in sunbathing or remain outdoors for prolonged periods with a false sense of security against sun-induced skin damage."[3]

Other Protective Measures

Besides using sunscreen, there are additional measures people with albinism and other fair-complexioned individuals can take to protect themselves from harmful sun exposure. These include paying close attention to the following factors:

Location: The closer you are to the equator, the more intense the sun is. Two hours spent in the sun in Key West, Florida, is more damaging than the same amount of sun time in New Hampshire under similar conditions.

Whether a person is at sea level or high in the mountains also has a bearing on exposure to the sun's **ultraviolet** rays. The National Organization for Albinism and Hypopigmentation cites that every 1,000 feet (305 m) you go above sea level increases the intensity of the sun's burning rays by 4 percent. The organization stresses that at 5,000 feet (1,525 m) above sea level, the sun's intensity is 20 percent greater.

Weather: The weather also influences the degree of skin damage caused by the sun. Bright days that are a bit overcast may fool people into thinking that the cloud cover will mask the sun's harmful rays. This isn't true, however. On such days, 60 to 80 percent of ultraviolet rays come through.

Time of Day: The time of day at which you are exposed to the sun is another important factor. The sun is most damaging between 10:00 A.M. and 2:00 P.M. Eastern Standard Time (11:00 A.M. to 3:00 P.M. Daylight Savings Time). Therefore, it's wise to limit sun exposure during those hours or take other precautions against burning.

Clothing: Wearing the right clothing can be an extremely helpful sun-protection measure. If it's cool enough, long-sleeved shirts are ideal. Hats with broad brims offer protection for the face and neck area. Dark-colored, tightly woven clothing offers more sun protection than light-colored, porous garments.

Although people with albinism need to guard against the sun's harmful rays, that doesn't mean they must remain inside and miss outdoor events and activities. With proper precautions, they can enjoy their natural surroundings and take part in the fun.

CHAPTER 3

HERMANSKY-PUDLAK SYNDROME

*M*ost people with albinism are essentially healthy. However, one unusual form of albinism, known as Hermansky-Pudlak Syndrome (HPS), can bring about several serious medical problems. Hermansky-Pudlak Syndrome is a rare type of albinism, chiefly characterized by excessive bleeding, colitis, lung disease, and kidney disease. The syndrome is not apparent when someone is born. An infant who has HPS looks like any other baby with albinism. However, HPS often proves to be present in a child who bruises easily and has frequent nosebleeds and bloody bowel movements.

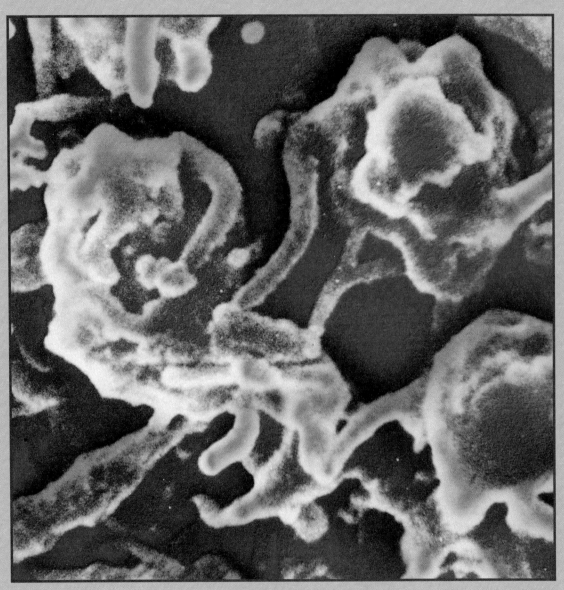

*This color-enhanced photograph shows
blood platelets beginning to bind together.*

Bleeding

The excessive bleeding caused by HPS is due to mal-functioning of the very small blood cells known as **platelets**. In someone who doesn't have HPS, these platelets bind together to stop a cut, scrape, or bruise from bleeding too much. But since the platelets of a person with HPS lack the necessary chemicals to remain bunched together, the bleeding continues.

In some children with Hermansky-Pudlak Syndrome, the tendency toward excessive bleeding is mild, so that HPS may not be immediately suspected. Other children with HPS, however, bleed quite heavily. Many of these young people have still another problem common to the syndrome. Besides having defective platelets, they lack a vital blood-clotting substance known as the von Wille-brand factor.

Intestinal Problems

Colitis, the inflammation of a person's large intestine, is another medical problem brought about by HPS. Colitis often causes the young person to have loose, bloody bowel movements and abdominal pain. In cases in which a great deal of blood is lost, blood transfusions or surgery may be necessary.

Lung Problems

Lung disease is also a problem for those with HPS. Many of these individuals develop **pulmonary fibrosis—**

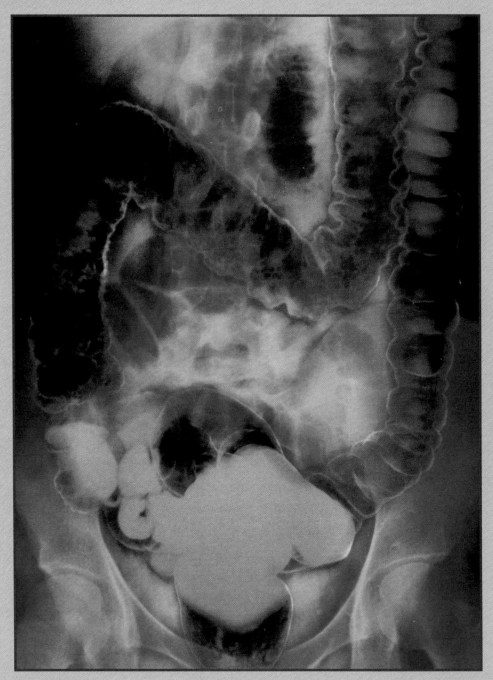

A false-color photograph of a large intestine (colored red) affected by colitis

a condition in which their lung tissues scar, limiting the amount of air taken in. This condition tends to worsen with time.

Hermansky-Pudlak Syndrome can be difficult to recognize. While one person may experience only slight bruising and mild bleeding, another may nearly die from severe hemorrhaging. However, everyone who has albinism should know about HPS. Since it is somewhat rare and varies so much among patients, not all doctors are familiar with it. Awareness of the disease may help a person with albinism to avoid a possible misdiagnosis.

CHAPTER 4

LIVING WITH ALBINISM

"Snowflake," "Whitey," "Old Timer"—these are just a few of the unkind labels sometimes thrust on young people with albinism. Those with oculocutaneous albinism (very light skin, eyes, and hair) readily stand out in a crowd, making them easy targets for ridicule and *scapegoating*. Such young people may be continually teased and asked humiliating questions like "Did you swim in a pool of Clorox?" or "Did you stop at a bakery before school and roll yourself in flour?"

Fact versus Myth

Unfortunately, our culture has created many myths about people with albinism. Though often ridiculous, these untruths have sometimes been wholeheartedly believed by people who either have never met a person with albinism or know nothing about the condition. People with albinism have been mistakenly viewed as ghosts coming back from the dead, sorcerers with magical powers, or even mentally retarded people.

Individuals with albinism have often been negatively cast by the media as well. Films, television shows, and books have sometimes portrayed them as serial killers, thieves, or aliens from outer space. Even the term "albino," once commonly used to describe someone with albinism, is demeaning. The word "albino" refers to a human being only in terms of a genetic condition—it implies that it is the individual's most important or distinguishing trait.

Yet this is never the case—human beings are too complex to be identified by a single aspect that has nothing to do with their intelligence, curiosity, sense of humor, artistic ability, or thoughtfulness. Therefore, when discussing a human being, the phrase "person with albinism" is preferred. The word "albino" should be used only in describing plants and animals. According to the National Organization for Albinism and Hypopigmentation, people with albinism may be immediately "noticed" by many, but truly "seen" by few. That makes it especially important that language not be used to limit or reduce human beings.

Self-Acceptance

Young people with albinism still grow up in a society in which their neighbors and classmates may believe the stereotypes about them. Feeling cut off and isolated from others their age and having different coloring than their family members can take a personal toll on them. At times, these unsettling emotions lead young people to deny or **minimize** their albinism. However, the condition is permanent, and until people with albinism are able to accept this, they will never feel comfortable with who they really are.

Accepting oneself can sometimes best be achieved with help from one's family and friends. Young people must feel free to discuss their feelings about having albinism. Also, the parents, grandparents, brothers, and sisters of someone with albinism must give up any damaging notions they might have about albinism and learn the facts. A little learning can go a long way in improving a difficult school or playground situation as well. It is sometimes helpful to have a parent or knowledgeable health-care professional address a class or auditorium audience on what albinism really is.

Having albinism can make you look different from your friends.

Brenda Premo, executive director of the Department of Rehabilitation for the state of California, is an outstanding role model for youths.

Support from Others

Young people with albinism, as well as older individuals, can also benefit from the work of the volunteer group National Organization for Albinism and Hypopigmentation (NOAH). NOAH holds workshops and conferences on albinism. Usually these undertakings include some programs specially geared to children and teens, such as puppet shows about albinism for young attendees and seminars on college planning for teens. In a workshop entitled "The Friendship Connection," parents develop "strategies for creating situations in which their children learn social skills and develop friendships."

Children with albinism must develop good coping skills to reach their fullest potential. This means learning when to confront someone who has made offensive remarks, and when it's best to just tune out that person. Some children with albinism have found that having a role model (a successful adult with albinism) to identify with can be a great confidence booster. Albinism has no effect on a person's ability to succeed in a profession—so, just like people of average coloring, people with albinism have become college professors, architects, preachers, doctors, computer scientists, psychologists, and much more. Seeing these individuals lead fulfilling lives reminds young people that sometimes a closed door can be pushed open with some effort.

Albinism in People of Color

Unfortunately, albinism can sometimes have an especially negative impact on young people of color. While African Americans have long been discriminated against by whites, those with albinism have often felt like outsiders within their own communities. Many people, unaware of the facts, find it hard to believe that two people of color can produce a child with light skin, hair, and eyes. Yet that's precisely what can occur if an African-American man and woman carrying the gene for albinism have a child together.

African Americans with albinism have cream-colored or light-brown skin; blond, reddish, or light-brown hair; and either blue or hazel eyes. Their precise coloring depends on the kind of albinism they have, but they are not always treated as if this were so. Instead, the birth of a baby with albinism frequently places a great deal of stress on an African-American family.

The child with albinism may be called cruel names at school and tauntingly told that his or her "real" father is white. Sadly, this may be just what some African-American fathers feel the first time they see a newborn with albinism. Even after learning the facts from a doctor or social worker, some men have still had trouble accepting a child whose coloring is so different from their own.

Many African Americans with albinism have light skin and blond hair.

Family Acceptance

Although this has been the experience of many African-American children with albinism, it hasn't been so for everyone. Some parents of these children look upon their newborn "golden child" as precious and special, and are in no way embarrassed by their baby's coloring.[1] In still other families, albinism is recognized and treated as nothing more than a genetic condition. Family members confidently explain why the child's coloring differs from other family members to those who question whether the young person belongs in the family. As with children of any race who have albinism, the African-American young people with albinism who do best are those who accept themselves.

CHAPTER 5

LOOKING AHEAD

*A*re people with albinism disabled? There is a great deal of disagreement in the medical community, as well as among those with albinism, about how this genetic condition should be regarded. There is no simple answer, because various forms of albinism affect individuals differently. In cases where a child's eyesight has been seriously diminished, he or she may be considered visually disabled. Under federal law, such young people are entitled to special school resources. The school's administration must create the "least-restrictive environment" to best meet that individual's needs.

Mainstreaming

Most students with albinism are **mainstreamed**—they attend general classes instead of going to a separate class for students with special needs. However, they may need some adjustments within the classroom. These might include having reading materials in large print or on cassette; being seated near the front of the classroom, as well as away from the glare from side windows; and working individually with a special-resource teacher who can help tailor the classroom situation to best meet their needs.

Though mainstreaming works for most children with albinism, it is not the best solution for everyone. Depending on the child's visual needs, personality, and classroom adjustment, other solutions can be explored. This might include spending part of the school day with other visually impaired students in a resource room, or perhaps attending a special school for visually impaired young people. In such situations it is important for the child's parents and educators to review the young person's progress and their goals for the student regularly. As no one way is right for everyone, the student's long-range best interests must be kept foremost in mind.

Sports

There is no reason why students with albinism cannot take part in sports during both physical-education periods and after school. The National Organization for

Many people with albinism, like this video editor, are successful professionals.

Albinism and Hypopigmentation notes that "small-ball" games such as tennis, badminton, softball, and baseball may be difficult for children with albinism due to the size and speed of the ball. However, such young people can do extremely well in sports like basketball and kickball, where a larger ball is used. Youths with albinism have also excelled in track, skiing, gymnastics, swimming, and horseback riding.

Bright Futures

While a person with albinism who has very poor eyesight might be viewed as having a disability, individuals with albinism have generally shown themselves to be extremely capable. Many have found that any problems albinism presented were usually easier to overcome than the widespread myths or **prejudices** about albinism. It is important for young people with albinism—or anyone who happens to look different from the majority—to remember that they are just as deserving and valuable as anyone else. People with albinism can succeed in even the most challenging professions, be loving spouses and parents, and lifelong friends. It is up to them to like and respect themselves—and society's responsibility to follow their lead.

GLOSSARY

ALBINISM a number of inherited conditions in which an individual either lacks or has a shortage of melanin, the substance responsible for the body's coloring

CARRIER an individual who has a gene that passes on a disease or trait to an offspring, even though the person does not have the disease or trait himself or herself

CHLOROPHYLL the green substance in plants that in the presence of sunlight converts water and carbon dioxide into food for the plant

GENES specialized structures in cells that determine which traits are passed from parents to children

INHERITED passed from parent to offspring through genes

IRIS the colored membrane surrounding the pupil of the eye

MAINSTREAMING placing disabled students in regular school classes

MELANIN the colored pigment contained in the skin, hair, eyes, and other tissues

MINIMIZE to reduce in importance or make light of

NYSTAGMUS an eye condition characterized by rapid, involuntary, side-to-side movements of the eye

OCULAR affecting mainly the eyes

OCULOCUTANEOUS of, relating to, or affecting the eyes and skin

OPTICAL AID a device designed to assist or improve vision

PIGMENT a natural substance that colors living cells or tissues

PLATELETS tiny particles found in blood that are essential for clotting

PREJUDICES unfair opinions formed in advance of or without examination of the available facts

PULMONARY FIBROSIS a disease characterized by a thickening of the tissue of the lungs

RETINA the membrane coating the back of the eyeball

SCAPEGOATING blaming a person for the misdeeds of another

STRABISMUS an eye condition characterized by a muscle imbalance ("crossed" or "wandering" eye)

SUN PROTECTION FACTOR (SPF) a number indicating the amount of protection a sunscreen provides from the sun's harmful rays

ULTRAVIOLET of or relating to the invisible light beyond violet in the light spectrum; ultraviolet rays from the sun can cause sunburn and eye damage

SOURCE NOTES

CHAPTER ONE
1. Benjamin A. Pierce, *The Family Genetic Sourcebook*
(New York: John Wiley & Sons, Inc., 1990), 3.

CHAPTER TWO
1. Virginia L. Small, "Vision and Albinism—One Person's
Description," *NOAH.News*, Spring 1996, 20.

2. James Haefemeyer, M.D., "Ask The Doctor," *NOAH.News*,
Spring 1966, 10-11.

3. NOAH, "Information about Albinism: Sun Protection,"
(fact sheet), 1989.

CHAPTER THREE
1. NOAH, "Information about Albinism: Hermansky-Pudlak
Syndrome," (fact sheet), 1989.

CHAPTER FOUR
1. NOAH, "Information about Albinism: African Americans and
Albinism," (fact sheet), 1989.

CHAPTER FIVE
1. "NOAH 1996 National Conference," *NOAH.News*, Spring
1996, 2.

ORGANIZATIONS & PUBLICATIONS

BOOKS

Adoff, Arnold. **All the Colors of the Race.** New York: Lothrop, Lee, & Shepard, 1982.

Brindze, Ruth. **Look How Many People Wear Glasses: the Magic of Lenses.** New York: Atheneum, 1975.

Feldman, Robert S. and Feinman, Joel A. **Who Are You? Personality and its Development.** Danbury, Connecticut: Franklin Watts, Inc., 1992.

Kelley, Alberta. **Lenses, Spectacles, Eyeglasses, and Contacts: The Story of Vision Aids.** Nashville, Tennessee: T. Nelson, 1978.

Le Shan, Eda, **What Makes You So Special?** New York: Dial Books for Young Readers, 1992.

Parker, Steve. **The Eye and Seeing.** rev. ed. Danbury, Connecticut: Franklin Watts, Inc., 1989.

Rahn, Joan Elma. **Eyes and Seeing.** New York: Atheneum, 1981.

Silverstein, Alvin. **Glasses and Contact Lenses: Your Guide to Eyes, Eyewear & Eye Care.** New York: Lippincott, 1989.

Stuart, Sandra Lee. **Why Do I Have to Wear Glasses?**
Secaucus, New Jersey: Carol Publications Group, 1989.

ORGANIZATIONS
The Albino Fellowship
16 Neward Crescent
Prestwick, Ayrshire, KA92JB
Scotland

The Albino Fellowship and Support Group
P.O. Box 717
Modbury, South Australia 5092

The Albino Support Group (Australia)
P. O. Box 123
Haberfield, N.S.W. 2045, Australia

The American Council for the Blind
1155 15 Street N.W.
Suite 720
Washington, D.C. 20005

American Foundation for the Blind
15 West 16th Street
New York, NY 10011

The Canadian National Institute for the Blind
National Division
1931 Bayview Avenue
North York, Ontario, M4G 4C8

National Association for Visually Handicapped
22 West 21st Street–6th floor
New York, NY 10010

National Organization for Albinism and Hypopigmentation
1530 Locust Street #29
Philadelphia, PA 19102-4415

The World Blind Union
58 Avenue Bosquet
75007 Paris, France

RESOURCES ON THE WORLD WIDE WEB

ALBINISM
Information on albinism, medical and other treatments, resources, and links.
http://www.stayhealthy.com/hrd/ME-TRRE_GEDI_Alsmhtm

ALBINISM AND HYPOPIGMENTATION
Information on albinism, Hermansky-Pudlak Syndrome and Waardenburg Syndrome, access to mailing lists, and links to other sites.
http://www.familyvillage.wisc.edu/lib_albi.htm

AMERICAN ACADEMY OF OPHTHALMOLOGY
Addresses and telephone numbers of organizations that offer information and services to people dealing with blindness or low vision.
http://www.eyenet.org/public/resources/res_sup_group.html

HERMANSKY-PUDLAK SYNDROME NETWORK
Information on the syndrome, its diagnosis and care, available services, and suggested reading.
http://www. medhelp.org/web/hpsn.htm

NATIONAL ORGANIZATION FOR ALBINISM AND HYPOPIGMENTATION (NOAH)

Offers WebBoards, information on albinism, events and publications, and links to related sites.

http://www. albinism.org

RESOURCES FOR PERSONS WITH ALBINISM

Bulletin describing agencies that offer services to people with albinism.

http://lenti.med.umn.edu/noah/resources.html

INDEX

Page numbers in *italics* indicate illustrations.

INDEX

ABOUT THE
AUTHOR

ELAINE LANDAU has a Bachelor of Arts degree in English and Journalism from New York University and a Masters degree in Library and Information Science from Pratt Institute. She has worked as a newspaper reporter, a children's book editor, and a youth services librarian, but especially enjoys writing for young people.

Ms. Landau has written more than one hundred nonfiction books on various topics. She lives in Miami, Florida, with her husband, Norman, and son, Michael.